United States and Saudi Arabia: Navigating Complex Relations with Yemen's Militias

How Yemen's Militias Influence Middle East Geopolitics

USSY UMAR

Contents

1

Intro

The Republic of Yemen is a nation located in the southwestern corner of the Arabian Peninsula. The landscape is predominantly mountainous and generally dry, although there are extensive areas where enough rainfall supports successful agriculture. The population primarily speaks different Arabic dialects and predominantly practices Islam. It is bordered by Saudi Arabia to the north, the Red Sea to the west, the Gulf of Aden and Arabian Sea to the south and Oman to the east. Of Yemen's 200 islands, the largest is Socotra, about 354km to the south of mainland Yemen.

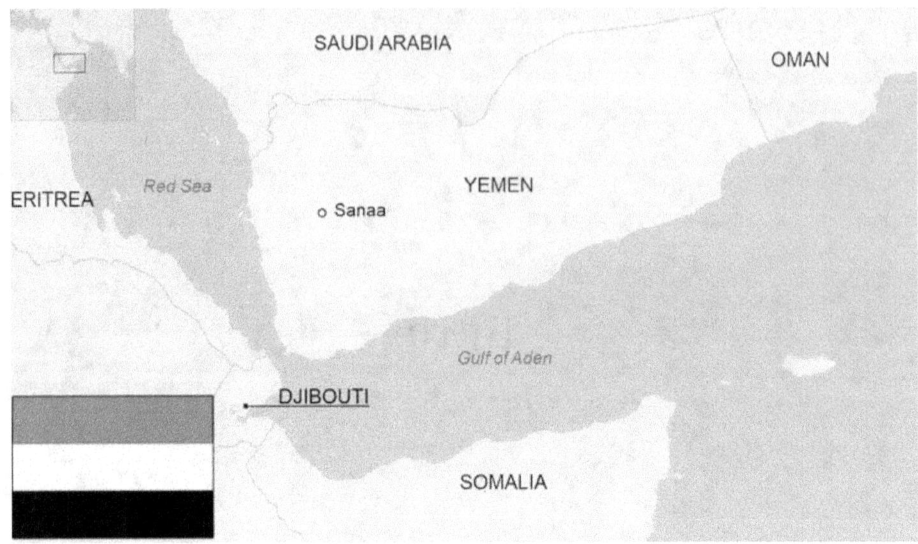

The Kingdom of Yemen, informally referred to as North Yemen, gained independence from the Ottoman Empire in 1918 and was established as the Yemen Arab Republic in 1962. Meanwhile, the British had established a protectorate around the southern port of Aden in the 19th century and withdrew in 1967, leading to the formation of the People's Republic of Southern Yemen, commonly known as South Yemen. Three years after its establishment, the southern government adopted a Marxist orientation and renamed the country the People's Democratic Republic of Yemen. The migration of hundreds of thousands of Yemenis from the south to the north fueled two decades of hostility between the two states, which eventually unified as the Republic of Yemen in 1990.

2

Yemeni unification

This story begins in the year 1990 when the Yemen Arab Republic in the north was united with People's Democratic Republic of Yemen in the south, forming the Republic of Yemen. Ali Abdullah Saleh from the north assumed the role of Head of State, while Ali Salim al-Beidh from the south became Head of Government. A transitional period of 30 months was established to finalize the unification of the two political and economic systems.

A presidential council was jointly elected by the 26-member advisory council of the Yemen Arab Republic and the 17-member presidium of the People's Democratic Republic of Yemen. The council appointed a Prime Minister, who then formed a Cabinet. Additionally, a provisional unified parliament was established with 301 seats: 159 members from the north, 111 members from the south, and 31 independent members appointed by the council's chairman.

In May 1990, a unity constitution was agreed upon and subsequently ratified by the public in May 1991. This constitution committed Yemen to holding free elections, maintaining a multiparty political system, upholding the right to private property, ensuring equality under the law, and respecting basic human rights.

3

The Zaidi Group

It all started with a group called Zaidi Shia Muslims who were members of a Shia Sect. The Zaydis, known as Fivers, represent one of the branches of Shi'a Islam. Zaydism is distinct from Twelver Shi'ia belief, which is practised in Iran and elsewhere, and is often said to bear more similarities to Sunni than to Shi'a Islam. The distinctions between Zaydism and Twelver Shi'a belief mean that Zaydis do not fall under the religious patronage of Iran, nor do they have the same cultural and spiritual links as some Shi'a communities elsewhere, in Lebanon for example. While all Shi'a confine the imamate to the lineage of Ali, different sects within Shi'a Islam differ on the genealogy, as to where to trace that lineage and where to terminate it. The Zaydis do so with Zaid bin Zain Al-Abideen.

The Zaidis, established an imamate in northern Yemen in the 9th century, which lasted for over a millennium, The Zaidi imams wielded both religious and political authority and maintained relative autonomy despite occasional external threats. The Zaidi imamate ended in 1962 when a revolution in North Yemen established the Yemen Arab Republic, leading to a period of conflict between royalists' supporters of the imamate and republicans.

Zaidi Muslim used to be the majority when the country was divided into two, but in the unified Yemen they became a minority and felt neglected and discriminated against. Post-revolution, Zaidi areas in northern Yemen, particularly Saada province, felt marginalised by the central government, dominated by Sunni Muslims. Economic neglect and political disenfranchisement contributed to growing resentment. Zaidi elites and religious scholars established the Al-Haqq (Truth) Party, aiming to promote the interests of the Zaidi community and counter the influence of Saudi religious ideologies within Yemen. This small political party, active in parliament from 1993 to 1997, strongly opposed the more dominant Islah (Reform) Party, which had close ties to Saudi Arabia and espoused Islamist principles. In 1997, President Ali Abdullah Saleh appointed Al-Haqq to the ministerial position overseeing religious endowments following a political disagreement with Islah.

In the 1990s, Hussein Badreddin al-Houthi, a Zaidi cleric who was a member of the Yemeni Parliament and also Al-Ḥaqq's most influential representative in parliament , resigned in protest and formed a movement called the Believing Youth Movement, promoting Zaidi revivalism and opposing perceived government corruption, and U.S. and Saudi Arabian influence.

Al-Houthi and his supporters were critical of the Yemeni government's perceived corruption, inefficiency, and lack of accountability. They believed that government officials were enriching themselves at the expense of the broader population, exacerbating poverty and inequality. Al-Houthi and his followers were staunchly opposed to what they saw as foreign interference in Yemen's affairs, particularly by the United States and Saudi Arabia. They viewed these external powers as undermining Yemen's sovereignty and perpetuating instability in the region. Yemen faced numerous socio-economic challenges, including poverty, unemployment, and lack of basic services. Al-Houthi's revolt was, in part, a response to these economic hardships, as well as the government's failure to address them effectively. As a Zaidi cleric, al-Houthi advocated for a revival of Zaidi Shia Islam and sought to protect the religious and cultural identity of the Zaidi community. The Houthi movement calls itself Anṣār Allāh ("Defenders of God") his movement promoted Zaidi teachings and traditions, emphasising the need to uphold Islamic principles in governance and society.

4

United States and the Houthi rebellion

After September 11, the U.S. declared war against terrorism. The escalating friction between the Believing Youth and the Saleh government expanded the organisation into a more inclusive movement. Saleh's endorsement of the United States' anti-terrorism efforts and the invasion of Iraq in 2003 sparked resentment among supporters of the movement. They perceived Saleh's backing of foreign interventions as akin to the historical disenfranchisement of the Zaidis in the 1960s, which had continuously posed threats to their cultural traditions and societal norms. Around that time, Hussein al-Houthi, attributing the hardships of his community to external influences, adopted a chant reminiscent of the "Death to America" slogan commonly associated with Iran: "God is great, death to America, death to Israel, curse the Jews, victory for Islam." As the movement gained momentum, the Saleh government intensified its crackdown on participants in June 2004, issuing an arrest warrant for Hussein al-Houthi. In September, following months of armed resistance, Hussein al-Houthi was killed by Yemeni forces. Leadership of the movement briefly shifted to his father and later to his brother Abdul-Malik.

Partially in response to the regime's harsh crackdown, the rebellion continued to expand and resisted attempts by third parties to negotiate a ceasefire. The movement's armament significantly increased, sourced primarily from the black market, defected members of the armed forces, and captured military stockpiles. (Iran's organized efforts to arm the movement emerged several years later.) The uprising in the north, followed by later unrest in the south, raised broader inquiries into the legitimacy of the Saleh government, the unity of Yemen, and the effectiveness of republicanism as a governing system for the country.

In early 2000, President Saleh signed a border demarcation agreement with Saudi Arabia and established friendly relations with the Saudi leadership. With this diplomatic progress, the Houthis lost their strategic value as a bargaining tool in regional politics. Despite having facilitated and tolerated their militarization, Saleh now desired for the Houthis to disarm. Subsequently, a series of conflicts erupted in northern Yemen. During this time, there were allegations of the Houthis receiving support from Iran. Additionally, Saleh faced accusations of lacking genuine commitment to decisively defeat them. Whenever the Houthis faced imminent defeat, Saleh would declare a ceasefire and engage in peace negotiations with them. Numerous theories have emerged to elucidate his tactics. One theory suggests Saleh orchestrated plots to undermine his cousin and adversary, Ali Mohsen. Mohsen, hailing from the al-Ahmar clan like Saleh, possessed considerable charisma and military acumen, presenting a formidable rival. As the commander of the first armored division in the Yemeni army, Mohsen was consistently entrusted by Saleh with leading operations against the Houthis.

Speculation suggests that Saleh may have sought Mohsen's demise in one of these conflicts. However, despite Mohsen often appearing poised for victory, Saleh allegedly intervened with ceasefire orders to halt the hostilities.

5

Houthi-Saudi Tensions

By late 2003, the Houthis had launched a full-scale rebellion against the Yemeni government from their northern stronghold, where they enjoyed local support. They blended in with civilians and utilized the rugged terrain of mountains and caves to conduct a guerrilla campaign against the better-equipped Yemeni Armed Forces.

It was at this time that the conflict went international, as the Houthis viewed Saudi Arabia as interfering in Yemen's internal politics. They believed that Saudi Arabia supported factions within Yemen that opposed them, thereby undermining Yemen's sovereignty. Saudi Arabia has been a strong supporter of the Yemeni government, particularly under Presidents Ali Abdullah Saleh and Abd-Rabbu Mansour Hadi, both of whom the Houthis have opposed. The Houthis see Saudi backing to suppress their movement and maintain control over Yemen through proxies. The Houthis follow Zaidi Shia Islam, while Saudi Arabia is predominantly Sunni and adheres to a strict interpretation of Sunni Islam (Wahhabism). The Houthis accuse Saudi Arabia of trying to impose its religious ideology on Yemen, threatening the Zaidi community's religious and cultural identity. In the year 2009, the Houthis crossed into Saudi Arabia amid their rebellion against Yemen's central government, killing soldiers and taking hostages. In response, For the first time, the Saudi army was deployed abroad without an ally. The Saudis conducted air strikes against the rebels and engaged in ground skirmishes, resulting in the deaths of more than 130 Saudi soldiers. The next significant round of Saudi-Houthi fighting began in March 2015. A coalition led by Saudi Arabia and the United Arab Emirates (UAE) launched airstrikes against Houthi targets in Yemen. The conflict between the Houthis and Yemen's internationally recognized government and its supporters continued to persist, despite U.N. efforts to facilitate peace talks.

6

Iranian influence in the Arabian Peninsula

Iran, watching from the sidelines, saw an opportunity with the Houthis fighting directly against their biggest rivals, Saudi Arabia. They began sending weapons to the Houthis, as implied by Saudi Arabia. The Houthis are often seen as being aligned with Iran, a regional rival of Saudi Arabia. Saudi Arabia views the Houthis as an Iranian proxy, and the conflict in Yemen as part of the broader Saudi Iranian rivalry for influence in the Middle East. Conversely, the Houthis see Saudi actions as part of a broader attempt to counter Iranian influence and suppress Shia groups in the region.

Tensions between the Saudi-led coalition and Iran escalated significantly on November 4, 2017, when a ballistic missile targeted King Khalid International Airport in Riyadh. The Houthis claimed responsibility for the attack, marking the first instance of a ballistic missile coming close to the capital since the conflict began. The Saudi Defense Ministry reported successfully intercepting the missile. Saudi Foreign Minister Adel al Jubeir labelled the attack as an act of war by Iran, asserting, "It was an Iranian missile, launched by Hezbollah, from territory controlled by the Houthis in Yemen." U.S. President Donald Trump also accused the Islamic Republic, stating, "Iran just took a shot, in my opinion, at Saudi Arabia… and our system intercepted the missile." Tehran dismissed the Saudi and U.S. assertions as "false, irresponsible, destructive, and provocative." Meanwhile, in Lebanon,

Hezbollah leader Hassan Nasrallah rejected the accusations against the group as "ridiculous" and "entirely unfounded." In reaction to the incident, Saudi Arabia implemented a nearly complete blockade on Yemen.

7

The Arab Spring

In early 2011, a wave of revolutionary protests and uprisings spread across the Arab world, reaching Yemen. Inspired by the successful uprisings in Tunisia and Egypt, Yemenis began to mobilize in January 2011. This movement triggered profound political and social changes in Yemen, a country already struggling with poverty, corruption, and instability. The Arab Spring's impact in Yemen was marked by widespread protests, political upheaval, and eventually, a devastating civil war.

Iran and Saudi Arabia viewed the Arab Spring as an opportunity to strategically choose sides in various countries, hoping to emerge with strong allies once the dust settled. One of their main focuses was Yemen, a country also experiencing an uprising. Protests erupted nationwide, with demonstrators demanding an end to Saleh's rule, greater political freedom, and improved economic conditions. The regime's response was brutal, with security forces frequently using violence to disperse crowds, resulting in numerous deaths and injuries. The situation escalated dramatically in March 2011 when government forces killed more than 50 protesters in the capital, Sana'a. This massacre galvanized the opposition and led to a significant increase in protests. Various political factions, including defected military leaders and influential tribal groups, joined the movement against Saleh, further weakening his grip on power. To quell the unrest,

13

Saudi Arabia sees the situation at their southern border and decide to step in with help of the United Nation, Convincing Saleh to transfer power to his vice president, President Saleh made several promises of reform and offers to step down, but these were widely perceived as insincere. The Gulf Cooperation Council (GCC) intervened, proposing a plan for a peaceful transition of power. After months of negotiation and continued violence, Saleh agreed to transfer power to his vice president, Abdrabbuh Mansur Hadi, in November 2011. This agreement granted Saleh immunity from prosecution; a controversial aspect that left many Yemenis dissatisfied with the new Saudi Arabia backed president. President Hadi's ascension in February 2012 marked a new phase for Yemen, but the transition was fraught with challenges. The Yemeni government remains weak and disorganized, while the Houthis are taking advantage of the conflict and popular uprising. They are seizing more territory from the government, bolstering their forces, and receiving increased support from their backer, Iran, which is supplying them with training, missiles, drones, and other advanced weapons. The fragility of the transitional government became evident as the Houthis, a Shia rebel group from northern Yemen, capitalized on the political chaos. By September 2014, the Houthis had taken control of Sana'a, and in early 2015, they declared a new government. President Hadi fled to Saudi Arabia, prompting a Saudi-led coalition to launch a military intervention in March 2015. This intervention aimed to restore Hadi's government but instead plunged Yemen into a protracted and brutal civil war.

The situation worsened significantly when the Houthis assassinated former President Ali Abdullah Saleh on December 4, 2017. Saleh had officially allied with the Houthis in May 2015, aiding them in gaining control over much of northern Yemen. However, the alliance was fraught with tensions. In August, one of Saleh's key advisors was killed after a clash with the Houthis. On December 2, Saleh publicly broke away from the Houthis, calling for a new relationship with the Saudi-led coalition. "I urge our neighbors and the coalition to halt their aggression, lift the blockade, reopen airports, and allow humanitarian aid and medical evacuations, and we will turn a new chapter based on neighborly relations," he stated. Two days later, he was assassinated by Houthi rebels in a roadside ambush. Iranian officials reportedly welcomed Saleh's death. Ali Akbar Salehi, Iran's nuclear program director and former foreign minister, commented that Saleh had received his due, as reported by Fars News Agency. A senior advisor to Supreme Leader Ayatollah Ali Khamenei remarked that Saleh's demise would enable the Yemeni people to determine their own destiny without Gulf interference. "The conspiracy of Saudi Arabia and the United Arab Emirates has been thwarted by the people of Yemen," stated Ali Akbar Velayati.

By 2017, the Houthis had gained complete control over the capital city, establishing their own government, and seizing military weapons, which helped them expand further into the south. Now in power, the Houthis run an oppressive regime that silences free speech, crushes dissent through arrest and torture, and recruit's child soldiers. Meanwhile, Saudi Arabia is becoming increasingly nervous as their southern border is now controlled by a group funded by their biggest enemy, Iran.

8

War with Saudi Arabia

The conflict between Saudi Arabia and the Houthis in Yemen had escalated considerably. The war started in 2015 when Saudi Arabia, under the leadership of Crown Prince Mohammed bin Salman, who was also the defense minister, spearheaded a coalition of Arab states to intervene militarily in Yemen. Their goal was to cut off support coming in from Iran and reinstate President Abdrabbuh Mansur Hadi, who had been overthrown by the Houthis. The Houthis, a Shiite rebel group with connections to Iran, had seized control of the Yemeni capital, Sana'a, and much of the northern region of the country.

While U.S. leaders are reluctant to become involved in another Middle Eastern conflict, they also aim to maintain a strong relationship with Saudi Arabia, a key security and energy partner in the region. Additionally, they are interested in curbing the growing presence of Al Qaeda in Yemen. Therefore, they provide logistical and intelligence support for the war. Ensuring Yemen's stability was crucial for U.S. national security interests due to its strategic location along key shipping routes in the Red Sea. Additionally, Yemen played a significant role in U.S. efforts to combat extremism, particularly against groups like Al Qaeda in the Arabian Peninsula (AQAP). Maintaining stability in Yemen aligned with U.S. objectives of safeguarding regional stability and addressing terrorist threats effectively.

The Obama administration provided substantial support to Saudi Arabia and its coalition partners in the Yemen conflict. This support included logistical assistance such as intelligence sharing, targeting support, and logistical aid to enhance the effectiveness of coalition airstrikes against Houthi targets and minimize civilian casualties. Additionally, despite concerns about the conflict's humanitarian impact, the U.S. continued to sell arms to Saudi Arabia and its allies under long-standing defense agreements, justified as necessary for Saudi Arabia's defense against external threats. Diplomatically, the U.S. consistently backed Saudi Arabia in international forums, emphasizing the coalition's right to defend Yemen's legitimate government and opposing Iranian interference in Yemen's internal affairs.

The U.S. backing of Saudi Arabia during the Yemen conflict under President Barack Obama highlighted the intricate nature of American foreign policy in the Middle East. Managing strategic partnerships, regional stability, counterterrorism goals, and humanitarian considerations presented considerable complexities. While the U.S. sought to bolster its allies and diminish Iranian influence, the Yemen conflict underscored the tough decisions and ethical challenges involved in handling international crises.

During Donald Trump's presidency, the United States continued to support Saudi Arabia in the Yemen conflict, but with notable differences from Barack Obama's approach. Trump maintained policies of military assistance to Saudi Arabia and its allies, which included arms sales, logistical support, and intelligence sharing to bolster their efforts against the Houthi rebels. His administration viewed Saudi Arabia as a crucial regional ally and a counterbalance to Iranian influence in the Middle East, framing support for Saudi actions in Yemen within a broader strategy of regional stability and containment of Iran. Unlike Obama, who faced substantial criticism for Yemen's civilian casualties and humanitarian impact, Trump encountered less public scrutiny on these issues. His administration placed less emphasis on humanitarian concerns, focusing more on strategic and security priorities. This approach reflected a shift towards prioritizing geopolitical alliances and perceived threats over humanitarian considerations in the context of Middle Eastern conflicts.

9

United Arab, A New war Front

The war in Yemen has involved multiple actors with shifting alliances and objectives, including the United Arab Emirates (UAE) and the Houthi rebels. The UAE's involvement, alongside Saudi Arabia and other coalition partners, has significantly influenced the war's dynamics and the broader regional balance of power. The UAE's actions are driven by strategic goals, such as countering Iranian influence, securing vital shipping routes through the Bab-el-Mandeb Strait, and combating terrorist groups like Al Qaeda in the Arabian Peninsula (AQAP). Additionally, the UAE has aimed to expand its regional influence through its military and political presence in Yemen. The UAE has played a pivotal role in the Saudi-led coalition, providing ground troops, air support, and logistical assistance. Emirati forces have been especially active in southern Yemen, including the strategic port city of Aden and along the western coast, where they have helped recapture territory from the Houthis.

In 2019, the UAE announced a drawdown of its forces in Yemen, shifting its strategy from direct military engagement to supporting local allies and focusing on counterterrorism. This move reflected a reassessment of its involvement in the conflict and the high costs associated with the war. Despite this drawdown, the UAE has continued to exert significant influence in southern Yemen through its local proxies and political alliances, notably the Southern Transitional Council (STC). The main goal of the STC is to secure greater autonomy for southern Yemen, with many members pushing for full secession and the re-establishment of an independent South Yemen. The STC asserts that it represents the interests of southern Yemenis, who have long felt politically and economically marginalized by the central government in Sana'a. The STC commands its own military units, referred to as the Security Belt Forces, which have been pivotal in the conflict in southern Yemen. These forces have participated in numerous military operations, frequently in collaboration with or supported by the UAE. This support has sometimes led to tensions within the coalition, particularly between UAE-backed forces and those loyal to President Hadi.

By late 2019, the war in Yemen had reached a peak of complexity. Saudi Arabia was supporting the internationally recognized Yemeni government, which was largely confined to the eastern part of the country. Meanwhile, the UAE backed the Southern Transitional Council (STC), a separatist movement in the south that was clashing with the Yemeni government. The Houthis, supported by Iran, maintained control over most major cities in the north. Al Qaeda and its allied militias continued to fight for control of small areas, and the US conducted airstrikes against Al Qaeda and ISIS while supplying more weapons to the Saudi-led coalition. Yemen was fracturing further, and hopes for peace required consolidating power. To address this, Saudi Arabia and the UAE reconciled their differences and jointly persuaded the Yemeni government and southern separatists to form a new coalition to unite against the Houthis. Despite these efforts, the Houthis, skilled in combat and equipped with Iranian missiles and drones, continued to strike Saudi targets, including refineries, threatening to increase global oil prices.

Later that year, the United Nations announced that approximately 20 million people in Yemen were dependent on humanitarian aid for their daily needs. The UN described Yemen as the world's worst humanitarian crisis, with over 24 million people, or about 80% of the population, requiring humanitarian assistance. The conflict had led to severe food insecurity, widespread malnutrition, and outbreaks of diseases like cholera. By this point, the war had settled into an uneasy stalemate. In April 2022, the UN brokered a ceasefire, bringing the fighting to a halt.

10

Road To Peace

Saudi Arabia and Iran had been engaged in behind-the-scenes diplomatic talks, sponsored by China. China initiated these high-level discussions, leveraging its longstanding relationships and economic partnerships with both nations. Chinese diplomats emphasized the mutual benefits of regional stability, particularly for economic development and security. They proposed economic incentives to both countries, highlighting how peace could enhance cooperation and investment opportunities in infrastructure, trade, and energy sectors.

China hosted a series of multilateral meetings, bringing together representatives from Saudi Arabia, Iran, and Yemen to foster dialogue, build trust, and address specific concerns of each party. These efforts culminated in an agreement that affirmed respect for the "sovereignty of states" and "non-interference in internal affairs." As part of the deal, Saudi Arabia reportedly agreed to push for less disparaging coverage of Iran by Iran International, a Persian-language satellite news channel. For years, Tehran had accused Saudi Arabia of using the channel to foment unrest. Although Iran International maintained its independence, it was reportedly funded by Saudi businesspeople and individuals linked to the royal court. The agreement also provided an economic boost. By March 2023, the Iranian rial had lost about half its value against the U.S. dollar since nationwide protests erupted in September 2022 following the death of Mahsa Amini in police detention. Within two days of the rapprochement announcement, the rial surged 12 percent against the dollar. By March 12, one dollar was trading for 438,000 rials on the open market.

China's successful mediation efforts enhanced its diplomatic stature and influence in the Middle East, showcasing its ability to act as a peacemaker and an alternative to traditional Western powers. By mid-2023, Saudi Arabia and Iran had officially restored diplomatic relations. Saudi Arabia hoped this would lead to Iran ceasing its support for the Houthis, thereby reducing attacks on Saudi Arabia's southern border.

11

The Return of the Houthis

In the fall of 2023, the Houthis gained international attention following the Hamas attack on Israel on October 7. Three days after this attack, Yemen's Houthi leader, Abdel-Malek al-Houthi, warned that if the United States directly intervened in the Hamas-Israel conflict, the Houthis would take military action. By mid-October, U.S. officials reported that the USS Carney had intercepted several Houthi cruise missiles and drones aimed at Israel. The Houthis continued to launch missiles and drones, officially entering the conflict to support Palestinians in the Gaza Strip on October 31. These attacks persisted into November.

On November 19, the Houthis hijacked a commercial ship in the Red Sea and subsequently attacked at least thirty-three other vessels using drones, missiles, and speed boats by late January 2024. Consequently, major shipping companies ceased using the Red Sea, which handles nearly 15 percent of global seaborne trade, opting for longer, more expensive routes around Southern Africa. This situation led to increased shipping and insurance costs, raising concerns about a renewed cost-of-living crisis. In response to the ongoing Houthi attacks in the Red Sea, the U.S. initiated Operation Prosperity Guardian, forming a coalition with 20 other countries, some of which preferred to remain anonymous. Saudi Arabia was notably absent from the list of participants, with Bahrain being the only Middle Eastern and North

African (MENA) country involved. The Biden administration re-designated the Houthis as a Specially Designated Global Terrorist (SDGT) group, reversing their delisting in 2021 which followed a last-minute designation by the Trump administration a month prior.

Houthi leader Abdul Malik al-Houthi declared that the group would escalate its attacks on Red Sea shipping if the aggression against Gaza did not cease and if aid and medicine were not allowed into the Palestinian territories. The Houthis claimed their first attack on cargo ships in the Indian Ocean, further expanding their reach as they continued attacks on Red Sea shipping. As of March 12, the Houthis had conducted over 60 attacks on both naval and commercial vessels in regional waters. These attacks increased following the launch of the US-led Operation Prosperity Guardian in December 2023. Peace talks remain stalled as Houthi attacks provoke international outrage. The Houthis also threatened Saudi Arabia, stating that if it allowed U.S. forces, specifically fighter jets, to use its territory and airspace for Operation Prosperity Guardian, they would target Saudi Arabia as well. Consequently, Saudi Arabia refrained from joining the US-led coalition and publicly urged the U.S. to "show restraint" in its response to Houthi attacks. In a separate development, AQAP leader Khalid Batarfi died this month from unknown causes, with Saad bin Atef al-Awlaki chosen as his successor. With new leadership and increasing instability and international focus on Yemen, experts predict a rise in AQAP recruitment and attacks.

It remains uncertain whether the Houthi attacks will cease soon, as they vow to continue their military operations until a ceasefire is agreed upon in the Gaza Strip and aid is allowed into the enclave.

12

References

- Arab Center Washington DC. (2021, March 19). A timeline of the Yemen crisis: From the 1990s to the present. Retrieved from https://arabcenterdc.org/resource/a-timeline-of-the-yemen-crisis-from-the-1990s-to-the-present/
- Arab Center Washington DC. (n.d.). A timeline of the Yemen crisis: From the 1990s to the present. Retrieved from https://arabcenterdc.org/resource/a-timeline-of-the-yemen-crisis-from-the-1990s-to-the-present/
- BBC News. (2018, June 19). Yemen crisis: Why is there a war? BBC News. Retrieved from https://www.bbc.com/news/world-middle-east-14704852
- Britannica. (n.d.). Houthi movement. In Encyclopedia Britannica. Retrieved from https://www.britannica.com/topic/Houthi-movement
- Britannica. (n.d.). Yemen - Agriculture, forestry, and fishing. In Encyclopedia Britannica. Retrieved from https://www.britannica.com/place/Yemen/Agriculture-forestry-and-fishing
- Brookings Institution. (2021, February 11). Who are the Houthis and why are we at war with them? Retrieved from https://www.brookings.edu/articles/who-are-the-houthis-and-why-are-we-at-war-with-them/
- Council on Foreign Relations. (2023, April 27). War in Yemen. Global Conflict Tracker. Retrieved from https://www.cfr.org/global-conflict-

tracker/conflict/war-yemen

- Department of Foreign Affairs and Trade. (n.d.). Yemen country brief. Retrieved from https://www.dfat.gov.au/geo/yemen/yemen-country-brief
- Editorial Board. (2021, November 9). Democrats are playing with fire. The New York Times. Retrieved from https://www.nytimes.com/2021/11/09/opinion/democrats-blue-states-legislation.html
- Minority Rights Group International. (n.d.). Zaydi Shi'a. Retrieved from https://minorityrights.org/communities/zaydi-shia/#:~:text=About%2040%20per%20cent%20of,branches%20of%20Shi'a%20Islam
- UNICEF. (n.d.). Yemen crisis. UNICEF. Retrieved from https://www.unicef.org/emergencies/yemen-crisis
- United Nations Yemen. (n.d.). About the UN. Retrieved from https://yemen.un.org/en/about/about-the-un
- Wikipedia. (2023, April 20). Hussein al-Houthi. In Wikipedia, The Free Encyclopedia. Retrieved from https://en.wikipedia.org/wiki/Hussein_al-Houthi
- Wikipedia. (2023, June 10). Houthi movement. In Wikipedia, The Free Encyclopedia. Retrieved from https://en.wikipedia.org/wiki/Houthi_movement
- Wikipedia. (2023, May 15). Yemeni unification. In Wikipedia, The Free Encyclopedia. Retrieved from https://en.wikipedia.org/wiki/Yemeni_unification
- Wilson Center. (2021, February 8). Who are Yemen's Houthis? Retrieved from https://www.wilsoncenter.org/article/who-are-yemens-houthis